American Sign Language

Animals

by E. Russell Primm III • illustrated by Kathleen Petelinsek

childsworld.com

The Child's World®
childsworld.com

Published by The Child's World®
800-599-READ • childsworld.com

Photography Credits
Clara Bastian/Shutterstock.com, cover, 3; Kurit afshen/Shutterstock.com, 1, 17; Helga Madajova/Shutterstock.com, 4; talseN/Shutterstock.com, 5; Rita_Kochmarjova/Shutterstock.com, 6, 11; Laurinson Crusoe/Shutterstock.com, 7; Petr Svoboda/Shutterstock.com, 8; MadisonRae/Shutterstock.com, 9; BIGANDT.COM/Shutterstock.com, 10; William Booth/Shutterstock.com, 12; Rudmer Zwerver/Shutterstock.com, 13; Volodymyr Burdiak/Shutterstock.com, 14, 15; tropicdreams/Shutterstock.com, 16; Dr.Pixel/Shutterstock.com, 18; Zebra-Studio/Shutterstock.com, 19; CHAINFOTO24/Shutterstock.com, 20; Minko Peev/Shutterstock.com, 21

ISBN Information
9781503888975 (Reinforced Library Binding)
9781503890053 (Portable Document Format)
9781503891296 (Online Multi-user eBook)
9781503892538 (Electronic Publication)

LCCN 2023950361

Printed in the United States of America

BRINGING THE WORLD
TO YOUNG READERS
19 68

Note to Parents, Caregivers, and Educators:
The understanding of any language begins with the acquisition of vocabulary, whether the language is spoken or manual. The books in this series provide readers, both young and old, with basic American Sign Language signs. Combining close photo cues and simple, but detailed, line illustrations, children and adults alike can begin the process of learning American Sign Language.

Let these books be an introduction to the world of American Sign Language. Most languages have regional dialects and multiple ways of expressing the same thought. This is also true for sign language. We have attempted to use the most common version of the signs for the words in this series. As with any language, the best way to learn is to be taught in person by a frequent user. It is our hope that this series will pique your interest in sign language.

A special thanks to our advisers: As a member of a deaf family that spans four generations, **Kim Bianco Majeri** lives, works, and plays among the Deaf community. **Carmine L. Vozzolo** is an educator of children who are deaf and hard of hearing, as well as their families.

E. Russell Primm III was a well-known figure in the publishing industry who produced thousands of acclaimed books for children. He was affiliated with organizations such as the American Library Association, the Chicago Book Clinic, and the University of Chicago Publishing Program Advisory Board.

Kathleen Petelinsek has loved books since she was a child. Through the years, she has written, designed, and illustrated many books for children. She lives in Wisconsin, near her granddaughter who also shares her love for books.

Cows stand up and sit down about 14 times a day

Cow

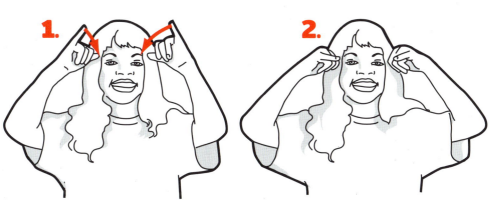

1. **2.**

Make the "Y" sign with both hands. Twist your wrists so your pinky fingers point downward. Repeat.

Horses can sleep standing up.

Horse

Make the "H" sign. Put your thumb on your temple. Bend and unbend your fingers two times.

1. **2.**

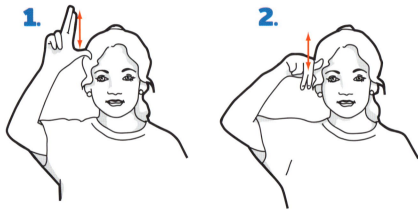

Pigs have a very good sense of smell. They can even smell things that are underground.

Pig

Place your flat hand under your chin. Bend and unbend your fingers (at the knuckles) a few times.

A group of goats is called a "trip."

Goat

Make a bent "V" shape. Touch your chin, then touch your forehead.

1.

2.

There are more than one billion sheep in the world.

Sheep

1.

2.

Make the letter "V." Pretend to clip hair as you move up your left arm.

A duck's webbed feet work like paddles to move it through the water.

Duck

Open and close your "bill" as if you are quacking.

1.

2.

Chickens can fly, but not very far.

Chicken

1.

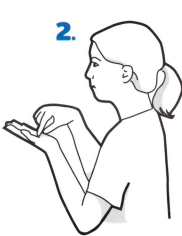

2.

Make a "beak" and bring it to your flat other hand (like a chicken pecking the ground).

Dogs can run about 19 miles (30.5 km) per hour.

Dog

Snap your fingers. Then slap the side of your leg as if calling a dog.

1. **2.** **3.**

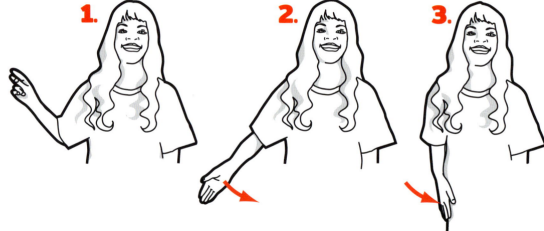

A cat can jump up to five times its own height.

Cat

1.

2.

Pinch and slide out like you are feeling cat whiskers.

Male rabbits are called "bucks." Females are called "does."

Rabbit

Make the "U" shape with both hands. Then flop your fingers like rabbit ears.

A mouse's tail is usually almost as long as its body.

Mouse

Touch your nose, then flick downward two times.

There are two types of elephants: the African and the Asian.

Elephant

Pretend to make an elephant's trunk.

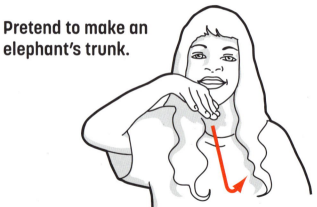

Giraffes can stand up to 18 feet (5.5 m) high.

Giraffe

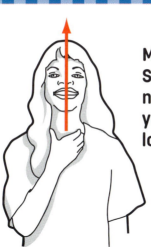

Make the "G" shape. Start at the base of your neck and move up over your head, showing the long neck of a giraffe.

Turtles live everywhere except Antarctica.

Turtle

Make a fist with one hand. Cover it with the other hand. Wiggle the thumb of your "fist" hand like the head of a turtle.

There are more than 4,700 different types of frogs in the world.

Frog

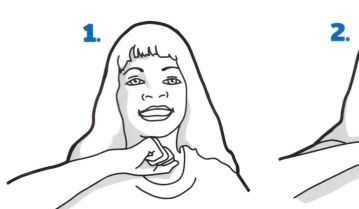

1.

2.

Make a fist under your chin. Flick two fingers out into a "V" shape a few times.

Snakes cannot chew their food. They must swallow it whole.

Snake

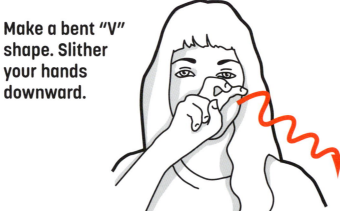

Make a bent "V" shape. Slither your hands downward.

Some snails can live to be 25 years old.

Snail

Move one hand across the other like a snail.

Butterflies fly about 12 miles (19.3 km) per hour.

Butterfly

Hook your thumbs. Then flap your hands like a butterfly's wings.

1.

2.

A bee only lives about 45 days.

Bee

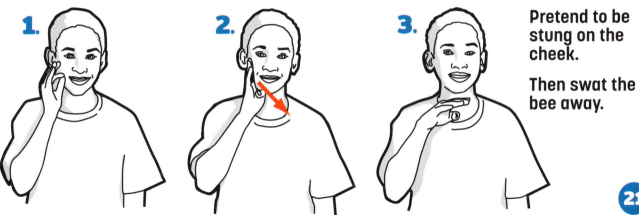

1.

2.

3.

Pretend to be stung on the cheek.

Then swat the bee away.

Wonder More

- How much did you know about American Sign Language (ASL) before reading this book? Do you already know some ASL signs? What new signs did you learn?

- Some words or specific names don't have signs. In these cases, you can spell the individual letters of the word, which is called fingerspelling. Look at the alphabet chart on page 23. Can you sign the letters in your name?

- With a partner, pick three signs from this book and practice them together. Are you able to understand each other? Is ASL easier or harder than you thought it would be?

- Do you think it is important to learn ASL? Why or why not? Where can you learn more signs?

Sign Language Alphabet

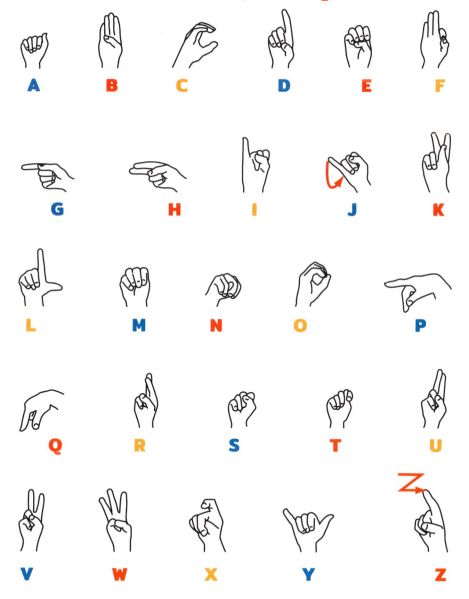

Find Out More

In the Library

Adams, Tara, and Natalia Sanabria (illustrator). *We Can Sign! An Essential Guide to American Sign Language for Kids*. Emeryville, CA: Rockridge Press, 2020.

Brakenhoff, Kelly, and Caterina Baldi (illustrator). *Sometimes I Like the Quiet (Duke the Deaf Dog ASL Series)*. Lincoln, NE: Emerald Prairie Press, 2022.

On the Web

Visit our website for links about American Sign Language:
childsworld.com/links

Note to Parents, Caregivers, Teachers, and Librarians: We routinely verify our web links to make sure they are safe and active sites. So encourage your readers to check them out!

A Special Thank-You!

Thank you to our models from the Program for Children Who are Deaf and Hard of Hearing at the Alexander Graham Bell School in Chicago, Illinois.

Aroosa is in third grade and loves reading, shopping, and playing with her sister, Aamna. Her favorite color is red.

Carla is in fourth grade. She enjoys art and all kinds of sports.

Deandre likes playing football and watching NFL games on television. He also looks forward to going to the movies with his family.

Destiny enjoys music and dancing. She especially likes learning new things and spends much of her time practicing her cursive handwriting.

Xiomara loves fashion, clothes, and jewelry. She also enjoys music and dancing. Her favorite animal is the cat.